Excel
Basic Skills

Handwriting

Year 1
Ages 6–7

Get the Results You Want!

Ada Munro & Ivy Morgan

PASCAL PRESS

ISBN 978 1 74125 734 2

Pascal Press Pty Ltd
PO Box 250
Glebe NSW 2037
(02) 9198 1748
www.pascalpress.com.au

Publisher: Vivienne Joannou
Edited by Rosemary Peers
Cover and page design by Sonia Woo
Typeset by lj Design (Julianne Billington)
Printed by Vivar Printing/Green Giant Press

Contents

Progress tracker

Colour each space object as you complete the matching practice page.

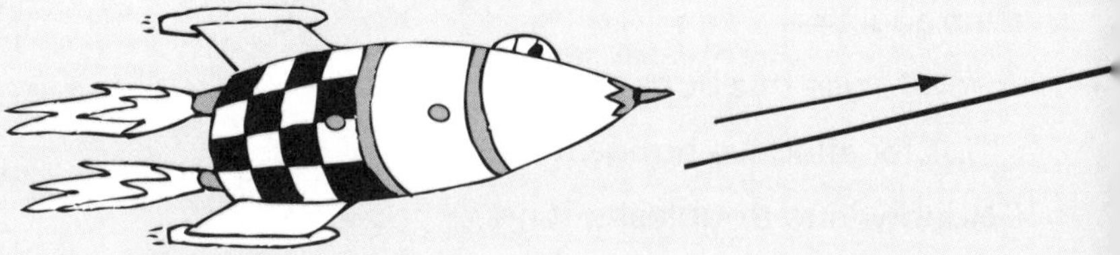

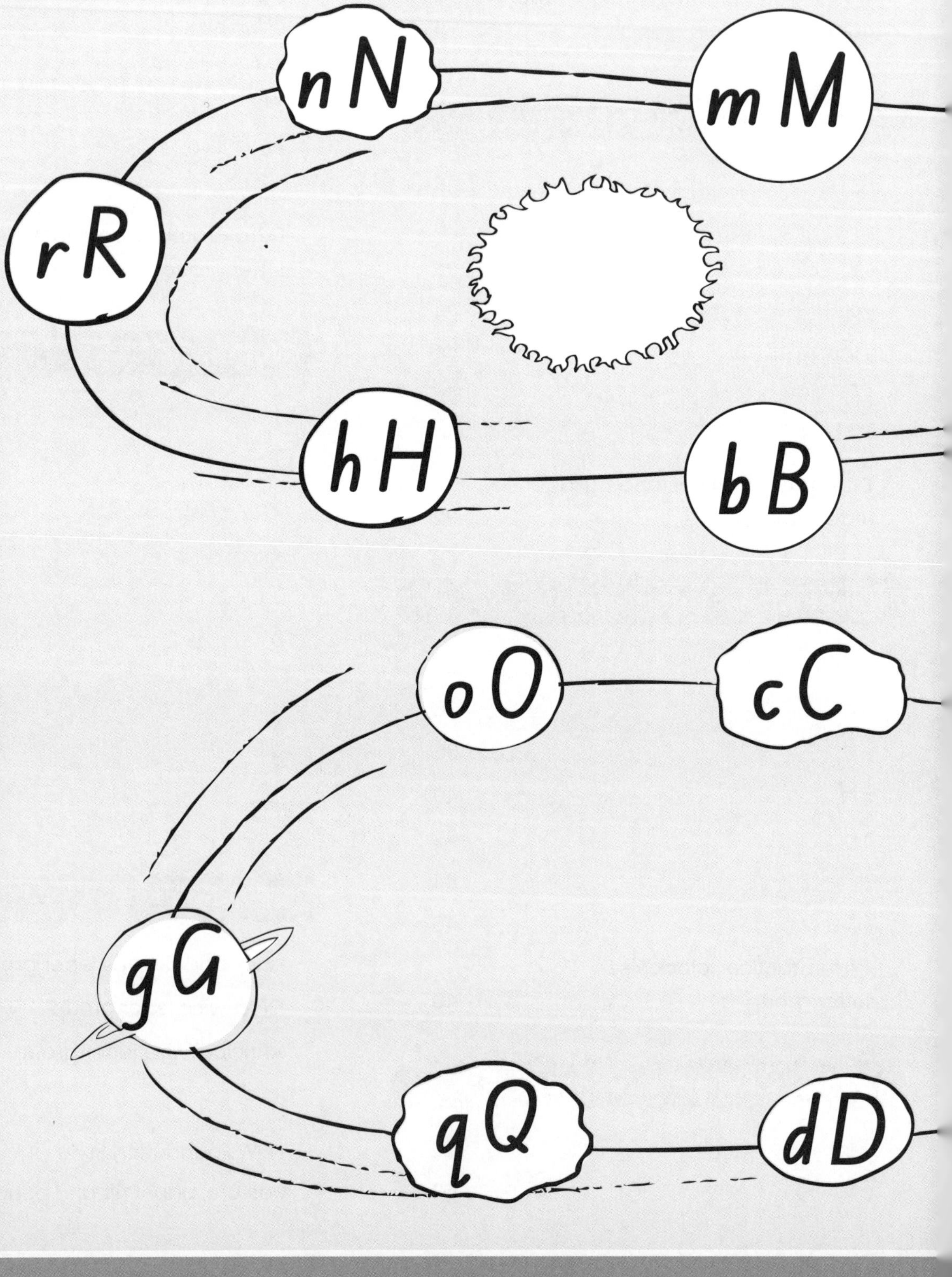

1
2
3
4
5
6
7
8
9
10

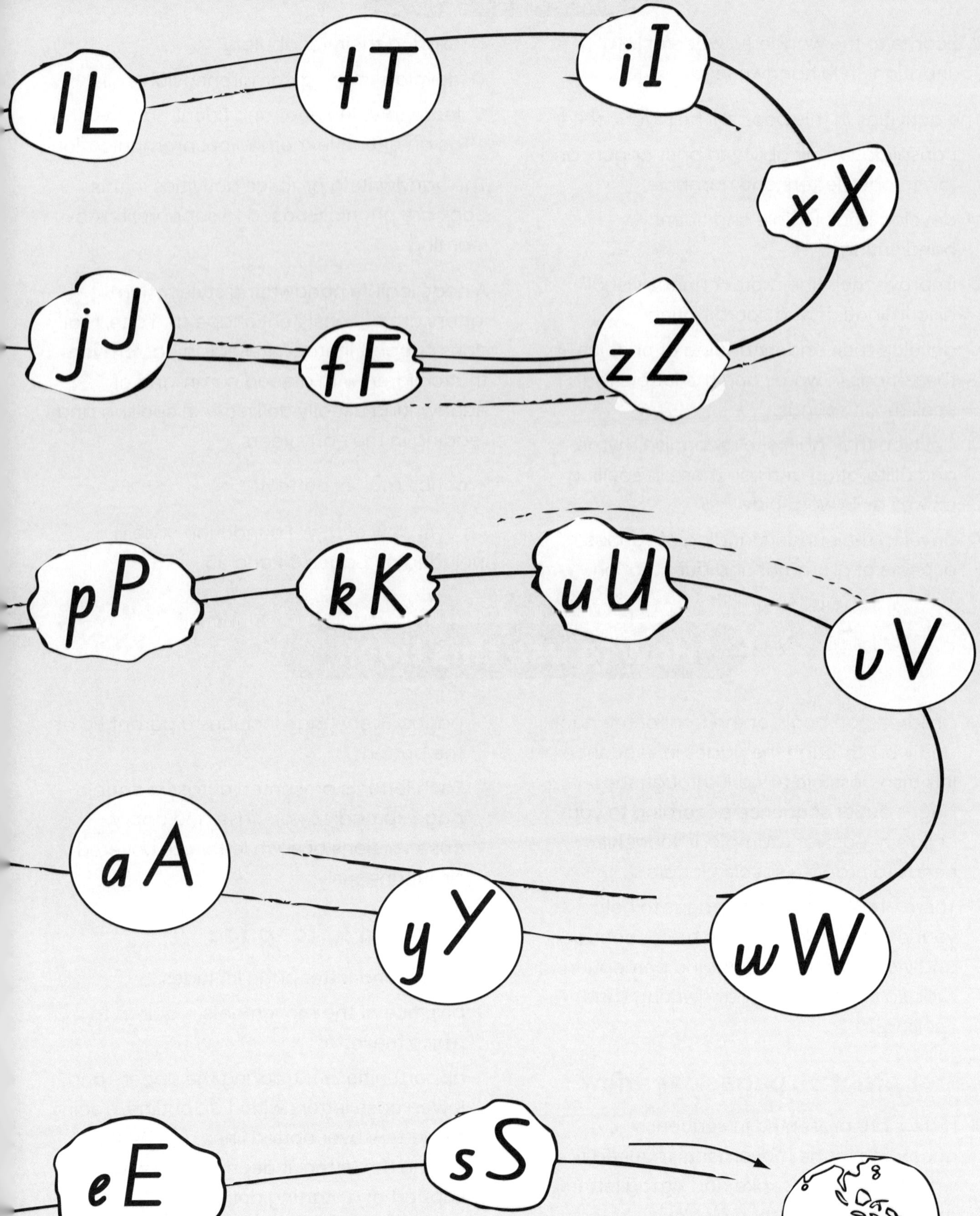
lL
tT
iI
xX
zZ
fF
jJ
pP
kK
uU
vV
wW
yY
aA
eE
sS

Introduction

Welcome to the wonderful world of NSW Foundation Style handwriting.

The activities in this book will help your child:

- consolidate their ability to print upper- and lower-case letters and numbers
- develop neat, legible and fluent handwriting
- improve their fine motor control, visual discrimination and coordination
- develop their understanding of phonics—the sounds in words and the letters that spell those sounds
- develop their ability to recognise rhyme and alliteration and use these in spelling as well as in word play
- develop their understanding of various aspects of grammar and punctuation
- expand their vocabulary
- develop reading comprehension skills
- learn to value neat and fluent handwriting as an effective method of communication.

The handwriting practice activities in this book are phonics-based to support literacy learning.

A neat, legible handwriting style, where letters are of consistent shape and size, really does support literacy. Research has proven that children with a good command of handwriting usually do better in spelling and reading in the early years.

Practice makes perfect!

An overview of NSW Foundation Style is included on pages 94 and 95.

How to use this book

- Children can begin at the front of the book and work through the pages in sequence. It is also possible to work through the pages out of sequence according to your child's needs; for example, if your child needs to practise specific letters.
- There are seven activity pages to help your child develop the fine motor control and visual discrimination and perception skills so important for handwriting (and spelling).

Letter practice pages overview

- Letters are presented in sequence according to the movements required to write them. Downstroke and zigzag letters are dealt with first, then clockwise letters and finally anticlockwise letters. The letter pages are followed by numeral practice pages. Every page includes a parent tip at the bottom.
- Each letter is presented across a double-page spread. Lower-case and upper-case versions of each letter are covered simultaneously.

Left-hand letter page

The left-hand letter page includes:

- practice of the movements required to make the letter
- opportunities for tracking the upper- and lower-case letters within an outline, tracing the letters over dotted lines and then writing the letters independently with the support of a starting dot
- a parent tip focusing on aspects of handwriting; for example, the letter

movements, the letter shape or a general reminder about body position, paper position, pencil grip, extra practice suggestions, and so on.

The tracking, tracing and independent practice activities make use of the guidelines on the page. Guidelines help your child learn to write letters of consistent size relative to each other. Start dots help with letter and word spacing, as well as showing the starting point of each letter.

Right-hand letter page

The right-hand letter page includes:

- Practice opportunities to write three words that follow a pattern such as rhyme (hot, pot, rot) or alliteration (quick, quack, quiet). The first row has students tracing the focus letter. The second row of three words has students writing the focus letter from a start dot and then tracing the rest of each word.
- Practice opportunities to write three words, most of which come from the top 125 common words that children need to learn. These words may not be able to be spelt phonetically; for example, time, they, what. They are also words that children need to learn to automatically recognise when they read rather than trying to sound them out. It has been found that children use these common words in their early writing.
- Practice opportunities to trace and then copy a simple sentence (a statement, question or command) from start dots. Children can explore the various sentence structures as well as the associated punctuation markers. The sentences reinforce the use of capital letters to begin sentences and the use of capital letters for people's names (proper nouns). Each sentence is also a reading comprehension activity in that there are two illustrations provided and children must colour the one that correctly matches the sentence.
- The parent tip on each right-hand page focuses on spelling, vocabulary, grammar, punctuation and the reading comprehension required to choose the correct illustration to match the sentence.

Extra letter practice

After each series of pages connected to a handwriting movement (straight lines and zigzags, clockwise and then anticlockwise) there are extra practice pages that focus attention on the movement similarities between the letters.

Numeral practice pages

Numerals 1 to 10 are introduced and practised in sequence. Zero (0) is taught on the page for 10.

Revision pages

These pages provide opportunities for students to consolidate or review their ability to write letters effectively in words. There are pages with activities for each of the three movements: lines and zigzags, clockwise and anticlockwise. The pages each have a labelling activity where students write the words without the support of any start dots or lines for tracing.

Progress tracker

The progress tracker on pages 4 and 5 is a quick reference that you can use to watch your child's progress through the letters and numerals. Your child can colour each space object or numeral that corresponds to a completed work page.

Tips for effective handwriting

- The poster on page 96 can be used by your child as a reminder for the three Ps of posture, pencil grip and paper/page tilt. It can also help them develop self-correcting skills.

The three Ps for right-handed writers

The three Ps are:

Posture

- Remind your child to sit with a straight back and with both feet flat on the floor.

Paper tilt

- The writing paper should be tilted correctly with the top right up. The left hand can hold the paper or book in place.

Pencil grip

- Reinforce a correct grip as early as possible in your child's life so that incorrect or awkward habits don't form in the first place. Tell your child to hold the pencil 2 cm from the tip between their index finger and their thumb with its shaft in the open web between index finger and thumb. The pencil rests on the middle finger. The heel of the writing hand rests on the page so the writing hand is steady.
- Use large soft-leaded pencils to begin with. Make sure writing implements are not slippery as these are more difficult to grip. You could also buy a rubber grip for your child's pencil. It can be used to help your child maintain a correct grip.

The three Ps for left-handed writers

- Ten per cent of people are left-handed and more boys than girls are left-handed.
- Being left-handed does not mean your child will have messy handwriting. It just means they will have a few extra challenges to overcome because the world is largely set up for right-handed people.

Posture

- Remind your child to sit with a straight back and with both feet flat on the floor.

Paper tilt

- Tilt the page left corner up and right side down so they can see the tip of the pencil and where they are writing. Tell them to use their right hand to hold the page steady. Use a start dot on the left side of the page to remind your child where to start.

Pencil grip

- Have your child hold their pencil 2 to 3 cm from the tip. This is close enough to the tip to give them good control of the pencil but far enough away from the tip that they can see their writing.
- Make sure the shaft of the pencil rests in the web of the hand between the thumb and forefinger.
- Left-handed writers have to push their pencil rather than pull their pencil, so it is more difficult. Pulling is smoother and easier than pushing. Pushing means you are more likely to tear the paper or smudge the writing.

- Tell your child not to press too hard. Buying them pencils with softer lead will also help prevent paper tearing. Softer lead allows for softer pressure and also helps avoid hand strain. Pencils with broader tips are easier than fine tips, which tend to tear the page more readily.
- Avoid marking pens with ink that stays wet because it can smudge as your child's hand moves over it as they write.
- The grip should be relaxed and not hooked or cramped. Make sure your child keeps their wrist straight. This will avoid cramping but also allow your child to see their writing. They need to keep their hand below the writing line.
- Practising on a vertical chalkboard or whiteboard can help free up arm movements.

TIP Check that your child's classroom allows for a left-hand computer mouse and left-handed scissors.

Sitting on the left

- In any situation where two children are sharing a desk or table for writing, the **left-handed child** should sit **on the left side** of the right-handed child so they don't bump arms when writing. Make sure there's space on the left to support the child's left arm.

Handwriting troubleshooting

- Handwriting is important for writing. When handwriting is slow and laboured, and when children have trouble reading their own handwriting, it leads to frustration and embarrassment at school. Children then avoid handwriting and it becomes a vicious cycle. Without practice they can't improve. Achieving success from the very beginning is important in supporting children's confidence as writers. Efficient handwriting helps students get their thoughts on to paper quickly and their creativity can flow. Most children can improve their handwriting with practice and targeted intervention but some may always struggle.
- Parents can help identify issues early on before children's self-esteem is affected to prevent the impact that poor handwriting has on other areas of learning.

IMPORTANT Do not despair if your child has poor handwriting. Your child can improve with practice. Make practice fun and rewarding and use other activities to support the various other skills that are beneficial for aspects of handwriting such as fine motor control and visual discrimination.

Watch your child as they write

- How do they look? Comfortable or uncomfortable? Relaxed or tense?
- What are their wrists, arms, shoulders, fingers, etc. doing as they write?

Look at the writing your child is producing

- Are the letters cramped, of irregular sizes or illegible?

Talk to your child about handwriting

- Ask them how they feel about writing. Do they enjoy it or avoid it? Do they value handwriting as a skill? If they find writing difficult, does it bother them? Are they worried about their handwriting? Do they care about handwriting? Have they seen you write to understand the importance of legible handwriting?

Handwriting problems can occur in these main areas:

Issue	What's needed	How to help
Speed and fluency	Too slow indicates that your child cannot write the letters without thinking; they are needing to concentrate to try to recall what they need to do.	Your child needs to develop automaticity (where writing letters and the letter sequences useful in phonics becomes automatic and they don't have to think about it).
Letter shapes and legibility	Muscle memory and automaticity Knowledge of where letters start and end and that letters in words are of uniform size; and that words need to be planned and their lengths estimated so they don't run into each other or run off the end of the line	Practise movements and the shapes. Practise identifying letters, their differences and similarities, including where each starts and finishes on the guidelines and its position in relation to the letter that precedes it inside words. Describe the letters as your child writes them to draw on auditory memory as well as visual and motor memory about where letters start and finish and their movements.
Letters not sitting correctly on lines	Knowledge about where each letter begins and finishes on the guidelines	Point out tall letters and long letters and which letters only have a body and no head or tail and where these aspects of the letters sit on the guidelines.
Slope	Understanding that a consistent slope is required so that letters do not run into each other or look cramped	Practise forming letters of consistent and regular slope.
Uneven and/ or inconsistent space between letters and between words	Understanding how letters are formed, especially anticlockwise letters so that enough space is left after a letter so that the following letter does not overlap it or encroach upon its space; for example, any letter followed by *o*, *a* or *e* Recognition that spaces exist between words and that, in English, writing moves from left to right	Practise writing and then reading what is written.
Mixing upper-case and lower-case letters	This is normal and just takes practice and the development of awareness and visual discrimination so that your child learns to recognise the differences.	Do activities to develop visual discrimination (see the activities on pages 11–17).
Reversals (writing letters and numerals back to front)	This is normal up until the age of about eight.	Use auditory and visual memory triggers; for example, tell your child that *b* looks a bit like a bat next to a ball. So for *b* say 'First the *bat* then the *ball*'.
Pencil grip and pressure	The correct grip is essential for relaxed and fluid writing. Pencil tips that aren't broken	Make sure pencils, paper or other writing surface is appropriate for your child's stage of development.
Posture or body position	Correct positioning of wrist, arm, neck and shoulders, feet and paper is necessary to avoid pressure, hand cramps, discomfort or neck strain.	Sit correctly (check the PPP poster on page 96). Do finger, wrist and shoulder warm-ups and stretching.
Inconsistent formation of letters	Impact on spelling	When letters in words look different each time a child writes them, it's hard for the child to develop any visual memory for the way the words should look or to develop any muscle memory for how it feels to write the word. This can affect your child's spelling.

Mighty maze

Help Matty find his way to Molly.

Going dotty

Colour the dots to match each pattern.

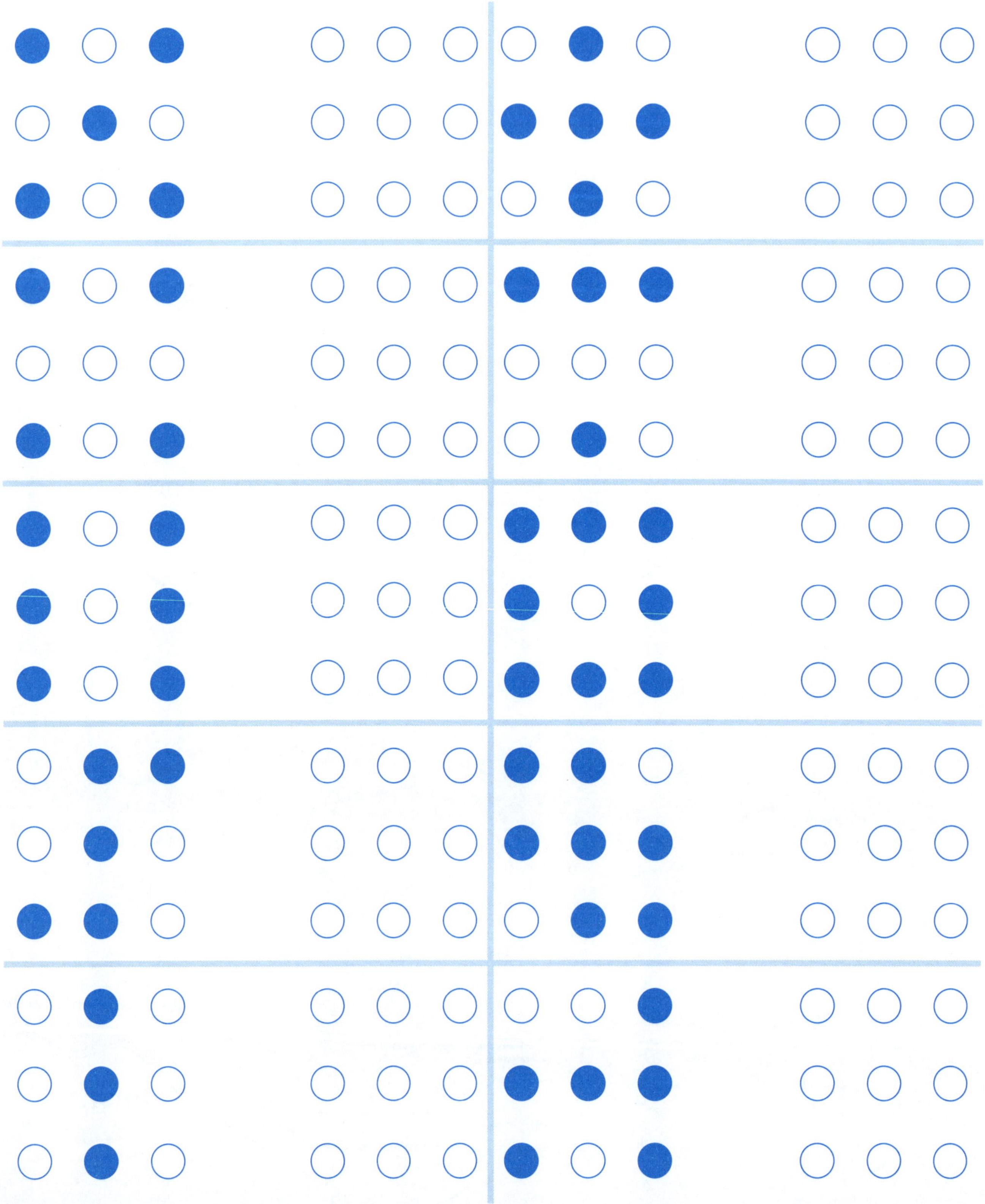

Look carefully!

Complete the pattern on each row.

—	—	—	/										
/	\	/	•										
\	○	/	\	○									
/	×	\	•	/									
•	|	•	|										
○	+	○	+										
○	/	/	○										
○	•	|	○	•									

Amazing maze!

Help the wombat find its way through the tunnels.

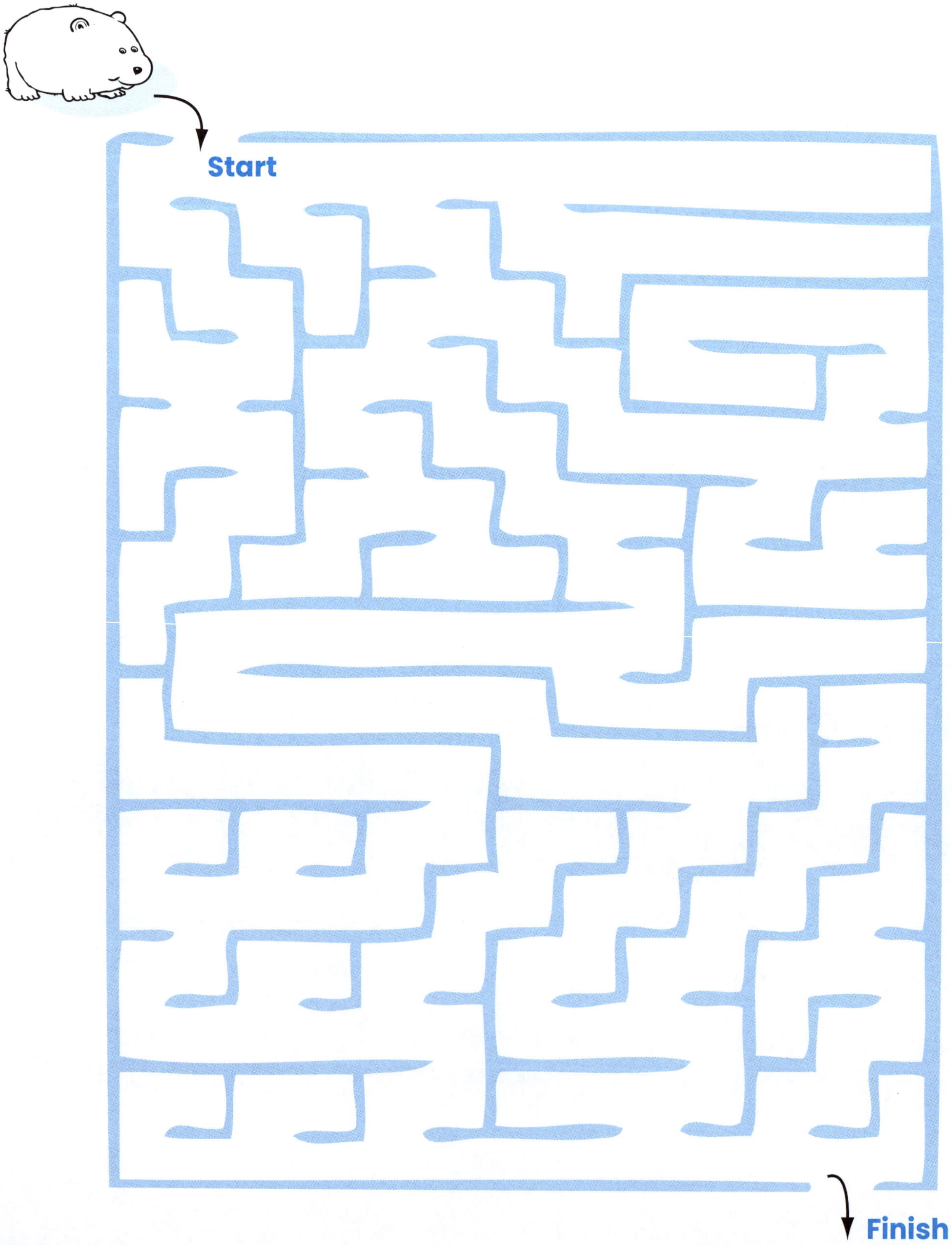

Look carefully!

Finish the pattern on each row.

+	—	○	○	+	—								
•	○	•	+	•	○	•							
—	/	/	—	\	\	—							
•	•	+	•	•	+								
|	×	+	×	|	×	+	×						
○	\	○	/	○	\								
•	○	×	•	○	×								
\	\	•	\	\	•								

Joining dots

Carefully copy each pattern.

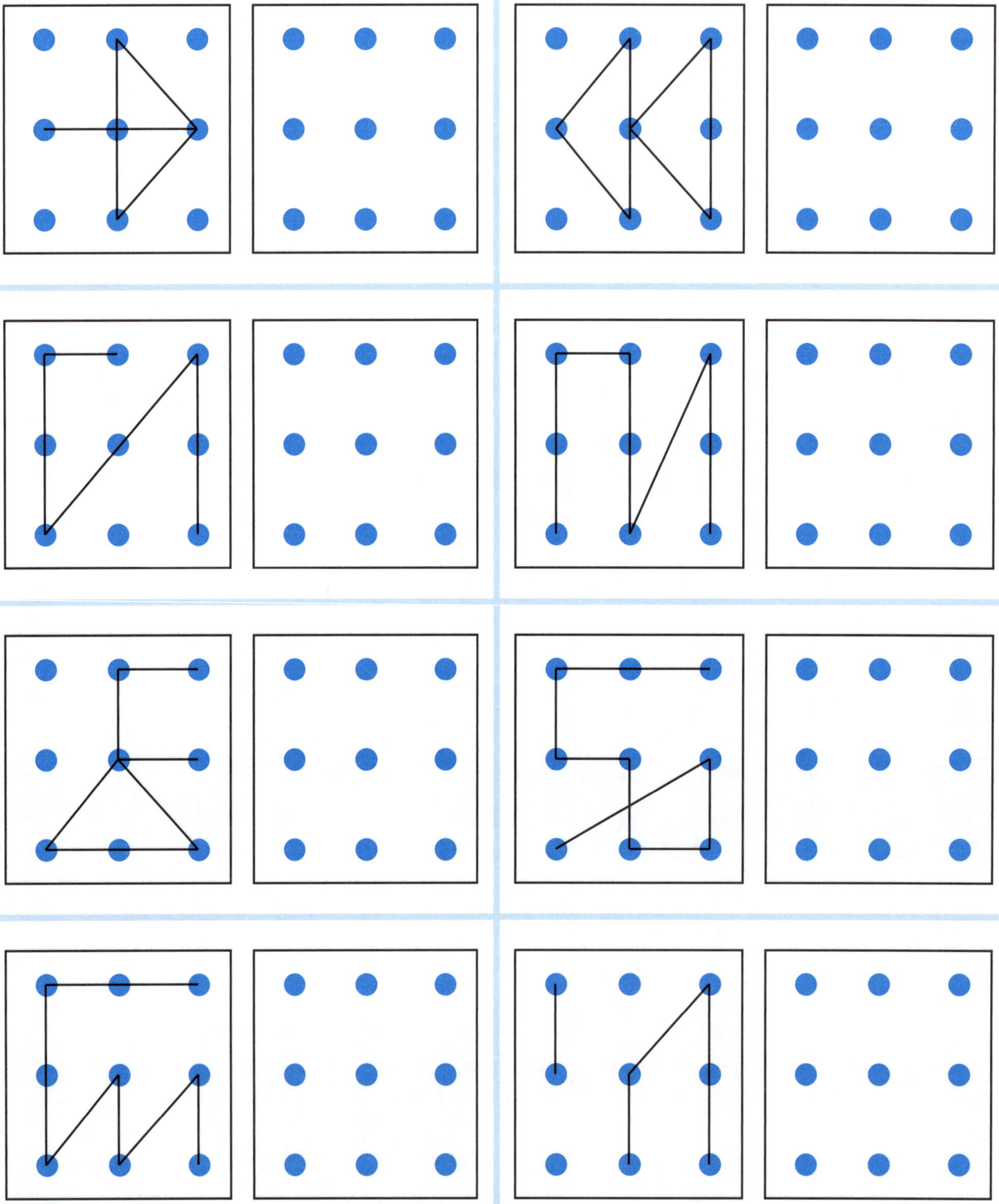

Copy this!

Carefully copy each pattern.

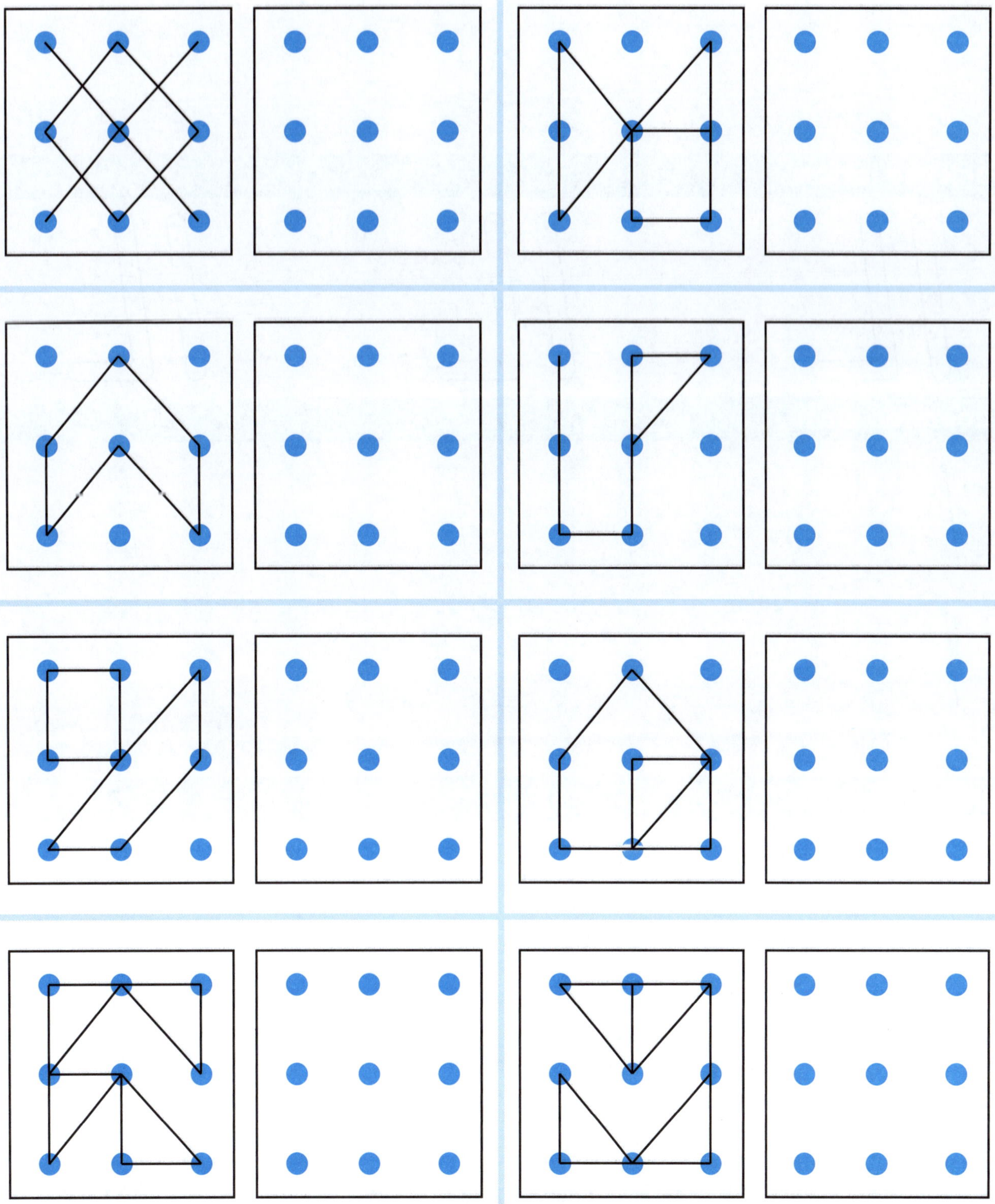

Practice

Trace

Track the letters.

Trace then write.

Trace then write.

PARENT TIP: Remind your child how to tilt the page correctly before writing. Watch that their pencil grip is correct. *l L* is a straight, tall letter. It starts at the top and moves down.

Trace each letter l.

ill hill fill ill hill

Write each letter l. Trace the words.

i hi fi i hi

Trace each letter l.

like little look like

Write each letter l. Trace the words.

ike itte ook ike

Trace then copy the sentence.

Look at the lion.

Colour the picture that matches the sentence.

PARENT TIP: Explore words that rhyme with -*ill* (*pill*, *till*, *gill*, *mill*, *still*). Discuss vocabulary for the illustrations: *lion*, *ladder*. The sentence is a command. Commands usually begin with an action (doing) verb, e.g. *Look*. Point out the sentence punctuation. Sentences begin with a capital letter. This sentence ends with a full stop.

Practice

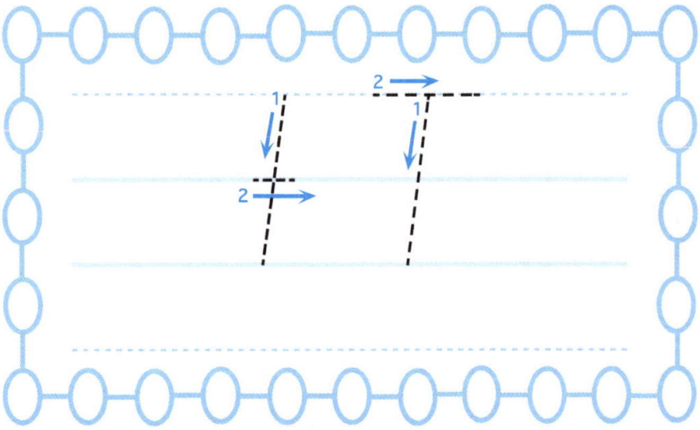

Trace

Track the letters.

Trace then write.

Trace then write.

PARENT TIP: Check your child's posture before they start writing. Lower-case t has a horizontal cross that sits on the line.

Trace each letter t.

rat bat that rat bat

Write each letter t. Trace the words.

ra ba ha ra ba

Trace each letter t.

these this then these

Write each letter t. Trace the words.

hese his hen hese

Trace then copy the sentence.

Take this tent.

Colour the picture that matches the sentence.

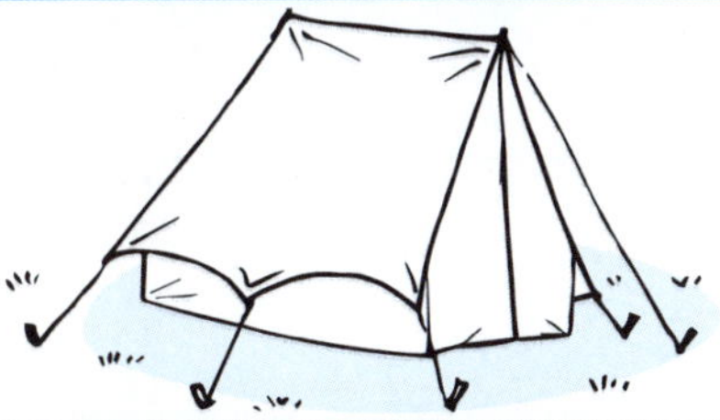

PARENT TIP: Explore words that rhyme with *-at* (*cat*, *sat*, *mat*, *fat*). Discuss vocabulary for the illustrations: *tent*, *table*. The sentence is a command. Commands usually begin with an action (doing) verb, e.g. *Take*. This sentence ends with a full stop.

Practice

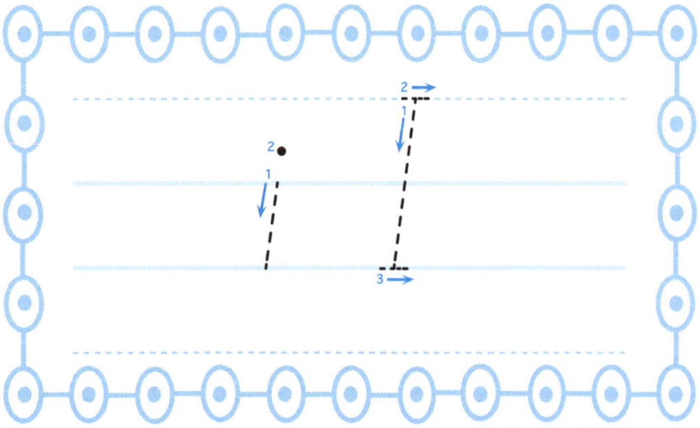

Trace

Track the letters.

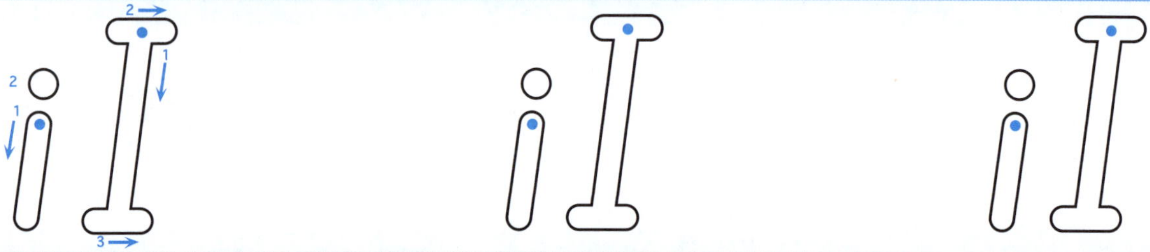

Trace then write.

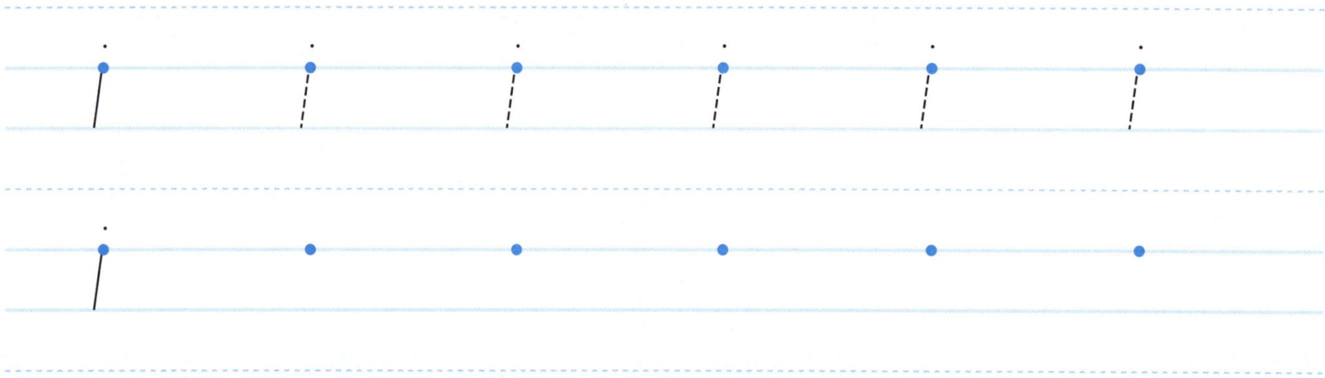

Trace then write.

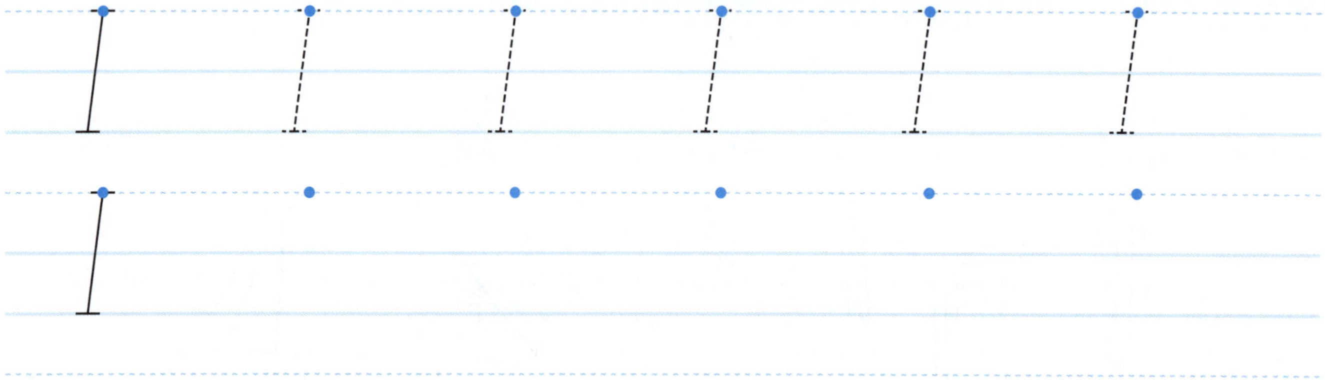

PARENT TIP: Remind your child to do some shoulder and arm warm-ups before starting the page. Upper-case *I* is a downstroke letter with top and bottom horizontal lines. These help readers distinguish it from a lower-case *l*.

Trace each letter *i*.

sit lit fit sit lit fit

Write each letter *i*. Trace the words.

st lt ft st lt ft

Trace each letter *i*.

I will into its I will

Write each letter *i*. Trace the words.

wll nto ts wll

Trace then copy the sentence.

Pig did a jig.

Colour the picture that matches the sentence.

PARENT TIP: Explore words that rhyme with *-it* (*pit*, *hit*, *mitt*, *nit*). Discuss vocabulary for the illustrations: *jig* (*dancing*), *sitting*. The sentence is a statement. It ends with a full stop.

Practice

Trace

Track the letters.

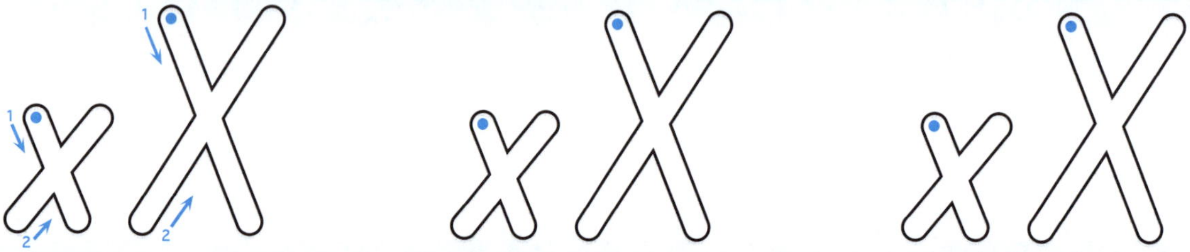

Trace then write.

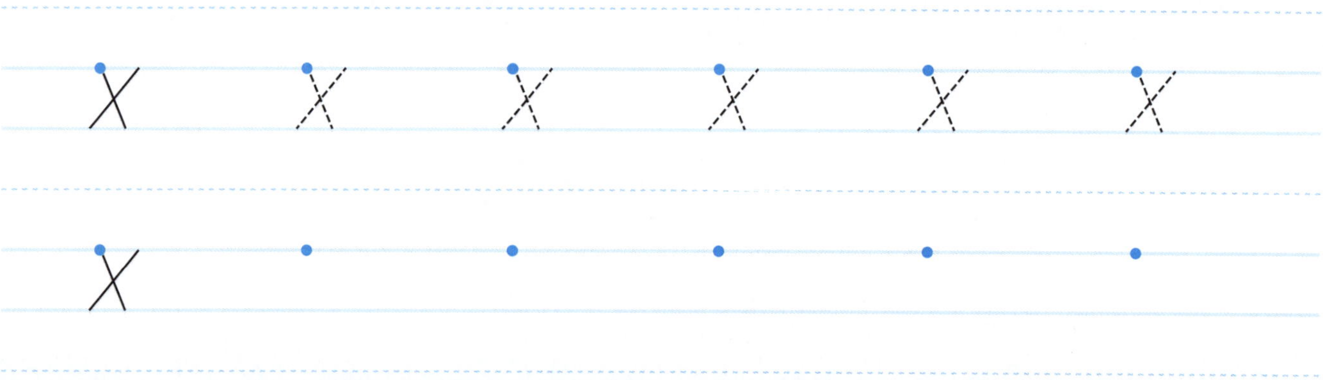

Trace then write.

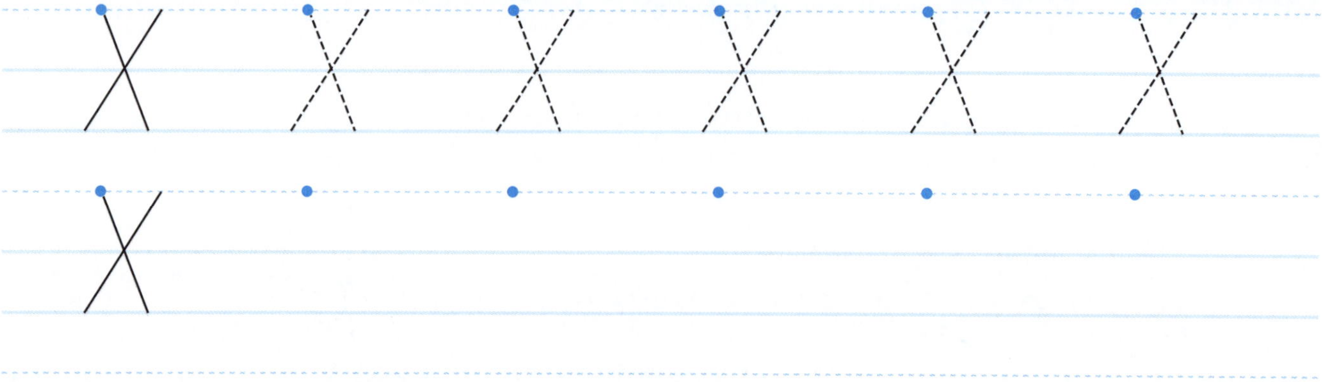

PARENT TIP: Watch that the second stroke on the *x* begins at the bottom and moves up diagonally towards the right.

Trace each letter *x*.

mix six fix mix six

Write each letter *x*. Trace the words.

mi si fi mi si

Trace each letter *x*.

axe sax sox axe sax

Write each letter *x*. Trace the words.

a e sa so a e sa

Trace then copy the sentence.

Fix the axe, Max!

Colour the picture that matches the sentence.

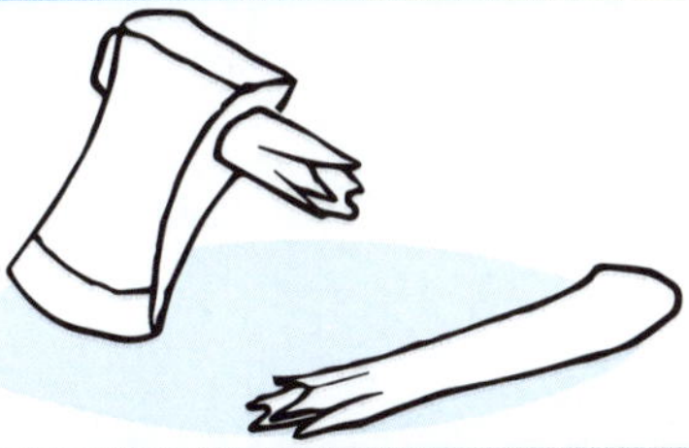

PARENT TIP: Explore words that rhyme with *-ix*. Discuss the difference between the middle sounds in *sax* and *sox*. Discuss vocabulary: *broken* (when you need to fix something the implication is that it is broken or not working properly). The sentence is a command. It begins with the action (doing) verb *Fix*. *Max* is a person's name. People's names are proper nouns. They begin with an upper-case (capital) letter. This command ends in an exclamation mark. It is said loudly or with emphasis or urgency.

Practice

Trace

Track the letters.

Trace then write.

Trace then write.

Parent tip: The two horizontal movements for Z begin on the left and move straight across to the right. Practise in the air with big arm movements before writing on the page. Point out that upper-case Z and lower-case z look the same but differ in size.

Trace each letter z.

fizz whiz frizz fizz

Write each letter z. Trace the words.

fi whi fri fi

Trace each letter z.

zoo zero zed zoo

Write each letter z. Trace the words.

oo ero ed oo

Trace then copy the sentence.

The bee buzzed.

Colour the picture that matches the sentence.

PARENT TIP: Explore words that rhyme with -*izz*. Discuss vocabulary: *bee*, *zebra*. The sentence is a statement. *Buzz* is an onomatopoeic word—it makes a sound. Make other sound words with your child: *swish*, *thwack*, *whoosh*.

Practice

Trace

Track the letters.

Trace then write.

Trace then write.

PARENT TIP: Upper-case F begins with a downstroke. Lower-case f begins on the right and moves anticlockwise before the downstroke. The cross is on the line.

Trace each letter *f*.

huff puff gruff huff

Write each letter *f*. Trace the words.

hu pu gru hu

Trace each letter *f*.

if find from if find

Write each letter *f*. Trace the words.

i ind rom i ind

Trace then copy the sentence.

Find the fox.

Colour the picture that matches the sentence.

PARENT TIP: Explore words that rhyme with -*uff* (*stuff, bluff, fluff*). Discuss vocabulary for the illustrations: *behind the bush*; *frog*; *fox*. Discuss positional language, e.g. words that tell where: *above, below, over, under, beside, between*. The sentence is a command. It begins with the action (doing) verb *Find*.

Practice

Trace

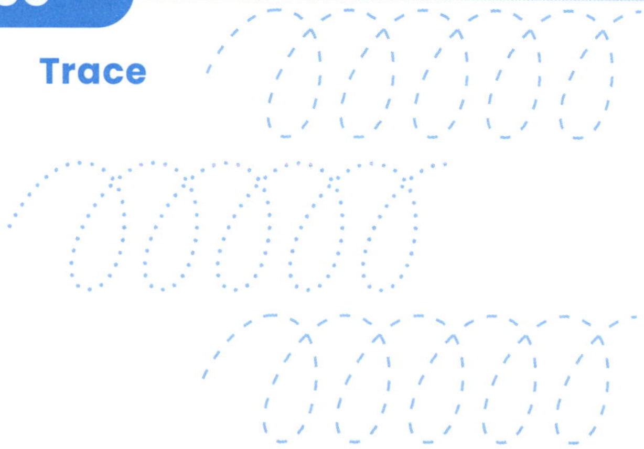

Track the letters.

j J j J j J

Trace then write.

Trace then write.

PARENT TIP: Have your child practise finger warm-ups and stretches before they start writing on the page. Lower-case j is a long letter. Upper-case J is a tall letter. It does not have a dot.

Trace each letter j.

jig jog jug jig jog

Write each letter j. Trace the words.

ig og ug ig og

Trace each letter j.

jelly jet jam jelly

Write each letter j. Trace the words.

elly et am elly

Trace then copy the sentence.

Jill just jumps.

Colour the picture that matches the sentence.

PARENT TIP: Point out that words in the top row begin with *j* and end with *g*. Only the middle vowel sound changes. Discuss vocabulary for the illustrations: *jumping*, *juggling*, *just*. Discuss what *just* means in the sentence. The action (doing) verb is *jumps*. *Jill* is a proper noun.

Extra practice: lines and zigzags

Trace each letter.

l t i x z f j

Write each letter.

l

t

i

x

z

f

j

PARENT TIP: Have your child check their own posture, pencil grip and paper position before they start writing.

Extra practice: lines and zigzags

Trace each letter.

L T I X Z F J

Write each letter.

L

T

I

X

Z

F

J

PARENT TIP: Check that your child's downstrokes are parallel.

Practice

m M

Trace

Track the letters.

mM mM mM

Trace then write.

m

m

Trace then write.

M

M

PARENT TIP: Have your child make clockwise circles in the air using big arm movements. Provide spare paper and practise writing clockwise circles, swirls and spirals. Upper-case M requires a pencil lift after the initial downstroke. Upper-case M looks like two mountains.

Trace each letter *m*.

mum hum drum mum

Write each letter *m*. Trace the words.

u hu dru u

Trace each letter *m*.

many them me many

Write each letter *m*. Trace the words.

any the e any

Trace then copy the sentence.

My monster mops.

Colour the picture that matches the sentence.

PARENT TIP: Explore words that rhyme with -*um* (*glum*, *plum*, *sum*). Discuss vocabulary for the illustrations: *monster*, *mouse*, *mop*. The sentence is a statement. It begins with a capital letter and ends with a full stop.

Practice

Trace

Track the letters.

nN nN nN

Trace then write.

Trace then write.

PARENT TIP: Lower-case *n* begins with a downstroke. The pencil is then kept on the page to bounce up and around to make a hill. Upper-case *N* requires a pencil lift after the first downstroke.

Trace each letter *n*.

tin pin win tin pin

Write each letter *n*. Trace the words.

ti pi wi ti pi

Trace each letter *n*.

no name new name

Write each letter *n*. Trace the words.

o ame ew ame

Trace then copy the sentence.

It is not a net.

Colour the picture that matches the sentence.

PARENT TIP: Explore words that rhyme with *-in* (*fin*, *bin*). Discuss vocabulary for the illustrations: *net*, *nest*. The sentence is a statement. It begins with a capital letter and ends with a full stop. Create spoken sentences with your child where you point to an object and state what it is not.

Practice

r R

Trace

Track the letters.

r R r R r R

Trace then write.

r r r r r r

r

Trace then write.

R R R R R R

R

PARENT TIP: Like lower-case *m* and *n*, the *r* begins with a downstroke. Keep the pencil on the page to trace up and then across. Upper-case *R* requires a pencil lift after the downstroke.

Trace each letter *r*.

car jar far car jar

Write each letter *r*. Trace the words.

ca ja fa ca ja

Trace each letter *r*.

ring rug run ring rug

Write each letter *r*. Trace the words.

ing ug un ing ug

Trace then copy the sentence.

Rain rusts robots.

Colour the picture that matches the sentence.

PARENT TIP: Explore words that rhyme with *-ar* (*bar*, *tar*, *star*). Discuss vocabulary for the illustrations: *rain*, *rusts*, *robots*, *rat*, *cloud*. Discuss the positional word *under*. The sentence is a statement. It begins with a capital letter and ends with a full stop. Discuss things that *rust* and why a *robot* might *rust*.

Practice

Trace

h H

Track the letters.

h H h H h H

Trace then write.

h h h h h h

h

Trace then write.

H H H H H H

H

PARENT TIP: Lower-case *h* is a tall letter that begins with a downstroke. Point out the similarities with lower-case *n*. Upper-case *H* has two parallel downstrokes with a cross bar to join them. The cross bar is on the line.

Trace each letter *h*.

hot hit hat hot hit

Write each letter *h*. Trace the words.

ot it at ot it

Trace each letter *h*.

her had him her had

Write each letter *h*. Trace the words.

er ad im er ad

Trace then copy the sentence.

Hen had a hat.

Colour the picture that matches the sentence.

PARENT TIP: Explore the initial sound /*h*/ in each word and the final sound /*t*/. The middle vowel has been changed from word to word. Ask your child to swap the final sound with a *g*, *p* or *d* or any other letter. Do you make any real words or only nonsense words? Discuss the illustration: the effect of the wind on the hat. The sentence is a statement. It begins with a capital letter and ends with a full stop. Make up proper noun names for the hen, e.g. *Harriet*, *Hetty*, *Henny Penny*.

Practice

Trace

Track the letters.

Trace then write.

Trace then write.

PARENT TIP: Practise in the air first. Lower-case *b* is similar to lower-case *h*. It begins with the downstroke and then bounces up to make a clockwise movement. The pencil stays on the page. Upper-case *B* requires a pencil lift after the downstroke.

Trace each letter *b*.

big bug bag big bug

Write each letter *b*. Trace the words.

ig ug ag ig ug

Trace each letter *b*.

be but been be but

Write each letter *b*. Trace the words.

e ut een e ut

Trace then copy the sentence.

Bring me the ball.

Colour the picture that matches the sentence.

PARENT TIP: Explore the initial and final consonant sounds in the words *big*, *bug*, *bag*, *beg*, *bog*. Only the medial vowel changes. Discuss vocabulary for the illustrations: *Bring*, *ball*, *book*. The sentence is a command. It begins with a capital letter and ends with a full stop. The action verb *Bring* starts the command.

Practice

Trace

Track the letters.

Trace then write.

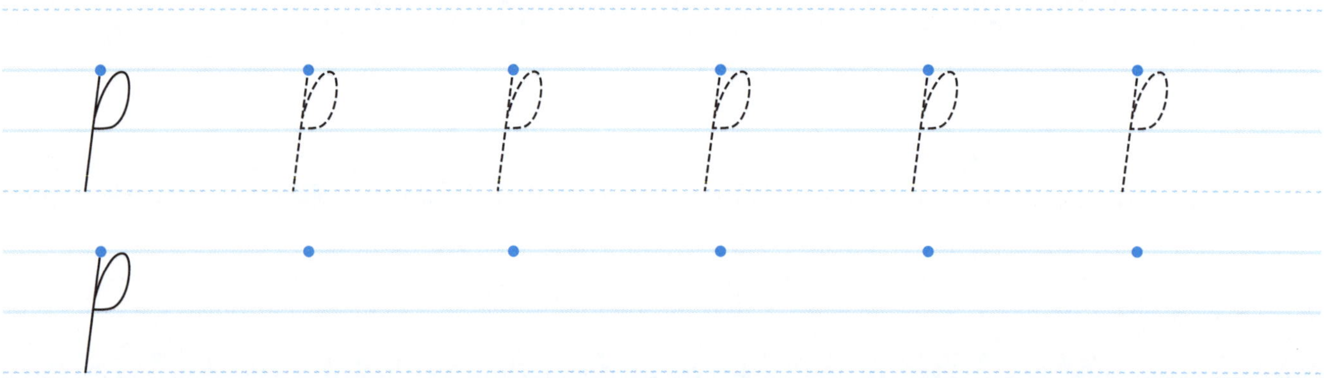

Trace then write.

PARENT TIP: Have your child do forward and backward shoulder rolls to loosen up and prepare for writing. Lower-case *p* is a long letter. It begins with the downstroke then traces up before moving clockwise and looping back to end at the downstroke. Practise on spare paper. Point out the similarities and differences between lower-case *b* and *p*.

Trace each letter *p*.

hop pop top hop pop

Write each letter *p*. Trace the words.

ho o to ho o

Trace each letter *p*.

part pick put part

Write each letter *p*. Trace the words.

art ick ut art

Trace then copy the sentence.

Pick a puzzle.

Colour the picture that matches the sentence.

PARENT TIP: Explore words that rhyme with *-op* (*bop*, *cop*, *lop*, *mop*). Discuss vocabulary for the illustrations: *Pick*, *puzzle*, *pieces*. The sentence is a command. It begins with a capital letter and ends with a full stop.

Practice

Trace

Track the letters.

Trace then write.

Trace then write.

PARENT TIP: Lower-case *k* is written without lifting the pencil. After the downstroke, trace back up before looping clockwise and back to meet the downstroke and make the final straight stroke. Upper-case *K* requires a pencil lift after the downstroke.

Trace each letter *k*.

kid kip kit kid kip

Write each letter *k*. Trace the words.

id ip it id ip

Trace each letter *k*.

take bake key take

Write each letter *k*. Trace the words.

ta e ba e ey ta e

Trace then copy the sentence.

Make a cake.

Colour the picture that matches the sentence.

PARENT TIP: Point out the final sound change in *kid*, *kip*, *kit*. Explore words that rhyme with -*ake* (*make*, *lake*, *brake*, *sake*, *flake*). Talk about the spelling of *key*. Words that end in *key* are *donkey*, *monkey*. Discuss the illustration. The sentence is a command. It begins with an action (doing) verb and a capital letter and ends with a full stop.

Extra practice: clockwise

Trace each letter.

m n r h b p k

Write each letter.

m

n

r

h

b

p

k

PARENT TIP: Look back over previous pages and ask your child to assess for themselves which letters need more practice. Use spare paper if necessary. Make sure your child is using pencil lifts at the correct part of letters.

Extra practice: clockwise

Trace each letter.

M N R H B P K

Write each letter.

M

N

R

H

B

P

K

PARENT TIP: All these letters begin with the downstroke and require a pencil lift. Ask your child to tell you which two don't begin the second stroke at the first dot (*H*, *K*). It's important that your child pays close attention to these visual differences and similarities in the same way that practising the physical movements develops muscle/kinaesthetic memory for the letter shapes.

Practice

Trace

Track the letters.

u U u U u U

Trace then write.

u

u

Trace then write.

U

U

PARENT TIP: Have your child use big arm movements to make anticlockwise movements in the air. Provide spare blank paper and have your child practise freely drawing anticlockwise circles, loops and spirals before starting this page. Lower-case u and upper-case U are written the same way except that upper-case U is a tall letter. They begin with the anticlockwise movement and end in a downstroke.

Trace each letter *u*.

nut shut jut nut jut

Write each letter *u*. Trace the words.

n t sh t j t n t j t

Trace each letter *u*.

up much just much

Write each letter *u*. Trace the words.

p m ch j st m ch

Trace then copy the sentence.

The pup runs up.

Colour the picture that matches the sentence.

PARENT TIP: Explore words that rhyme with -*ut* (*tut*, *gut*, *cut*). Discuss vocabulary: *dog*/*pup*, *up*/*down*. Point out the /*ch*/ sound at the end of *much*. Think of other words that end in /*ch*/ (*such*, *crutch*, *hutch*). For the illustration, discuss positional language as well as opposites. Have fun with opposites: *up*/*down*, *hot*/*cold*, *good*/*bad*, *under*/*over*, *big*/*little*, etc. The sentence is a statement. It begins with a capital letter and ends with a full stop.

Practice

Trace

Track the letters.

Trace then write.

Trace then write.

PARENT TIP: Have your child check their own posture, pencil grip and paper position before they begin writing. Ask your child to tell you the similarities and differences between the lower-case *v* and the upper-case *V* before they start this page.

Trace each letter v.

vet vat vim vet vat

Write each letter v. Trace the words.

et at im et at

Trace each letter v.

very love van very

Write each letter v. Trace the words.

ery lo e an ery

Trace then copy the sentence.

Viv is a vet.

Colour the picture that matches the sentence.

PARENT TIP: Scramble the letters to make three-letter words. Start with *vet* and change *e* to *a* to make *vat*. Change *a* to *i* to make *vit*, then change *t* to *m* to make *vim*. Sound out each word. Discuss real and nonsense words. Change *v* to *p* to make *pet*, and so on. Discuss vocabulary for the illustrations (*vet*, *firefighter*) and other words for jobs people do (*baker*, *chef*, *gardener*, *doctor*, *nurse*). The sentence is a statement. It begins with a capital letter and ends with a full stop. Point out that *Viv* is often a girl's name which can be short for *Vivienne*.

Practice

Trace

Track the letters.

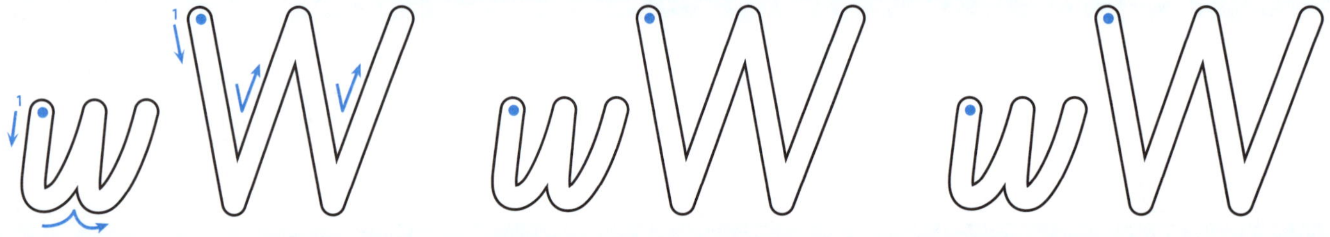

Trace then write.

Trace then write.

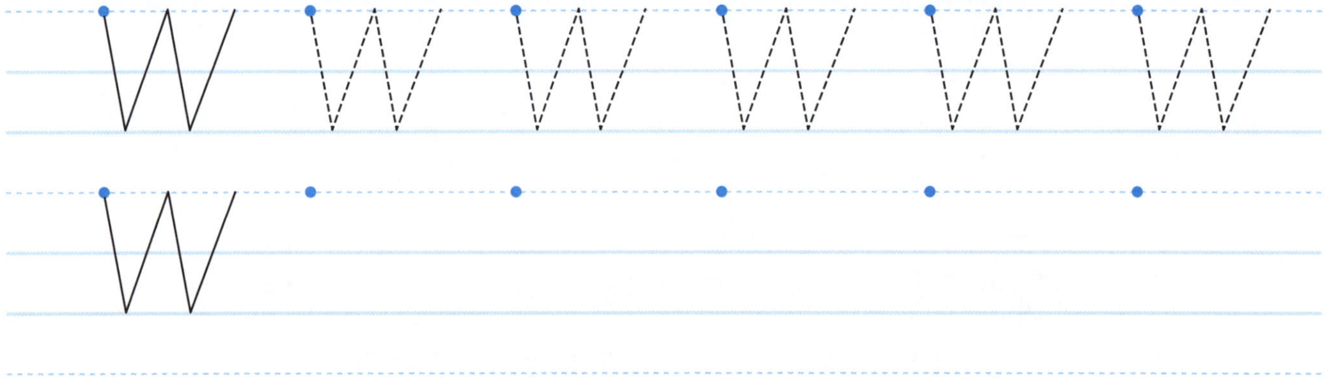

PARENT TIP: Remind your child to relax their neck, wrist and shoulders. Point out that W and w begin the same way as U and u. Have your child use spare blank paper to practise the letters before writing between the lines on this page.

Trace each letter *w*.

wig wax web wig

Write each letter *w*. Trace the words.

ig ax eb ig

Trace each letter *w*.

what which we what

Write each letter *w*. Trace the words.

hat hich e hat

Trace then copy the sentence.

Wally has a wig.

Colour the picture that matches the sentence.

PARENT TIP: Explore three-letter (consonant, vowel, consonant) words using scrabble tiles. The words *what* and *which* are often used to begin questions. Ask your child to think of some questions starting with either *which* or *what*; for example, *What time is it?* Discuss vocabulary for the illustrations: *walrus*, *wig*, *water*. The sentence is a statement. It begins with a capital letter and ends with a full stop.

Practice

Trace

Track the letters.

y Y y Y y Y

Trace then write.

y

y

Trace then write.

Y

Y

PARENT TIP: Lower-case y starts like a lower-case u but finishes with a long tail rather than a downstroke. Upper-case Y is a tall letter that needs a pencil lift.

Trace each letter y.

day ray pay day ray

Write each letter y. Trace the words.

da ra pa da ra

Trace each letter y.

your yell yet yell yet

Write each letter y. Trace the words.

our ell et ell et

Trace then copy the sentence.

Is it a yak? Yes!

Colour the picture that matches the sentence.

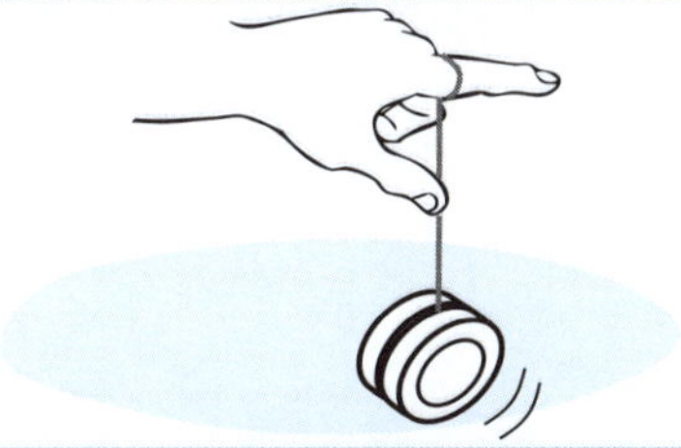

PARENT TIP: Explore words that rhyme with -*ay*. Discuss vocabulary for the illustrations: *yoyo*, *yak*. The sentence is a question. It begins with a capital letter and ends with a question mark. Other common words used to start questions include *What*, *Where*, *When*, *Why*, *How*, *Who*. Make up questions with your child. Write them. Use a question mark at the end of each one.

Practice

Trace

Track the letters.

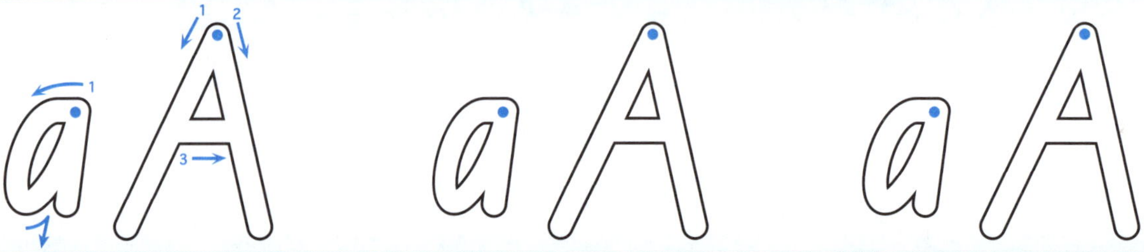

Trace then write.

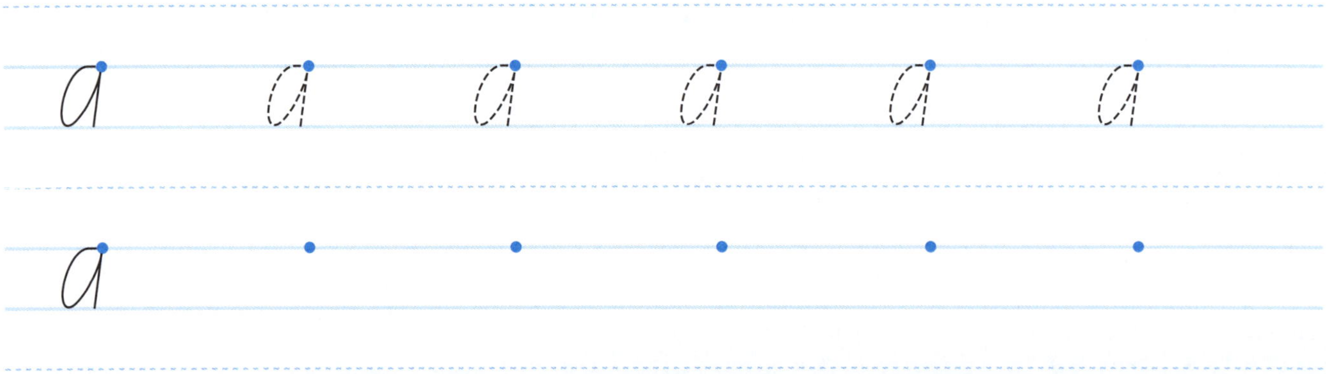

Trace then write.

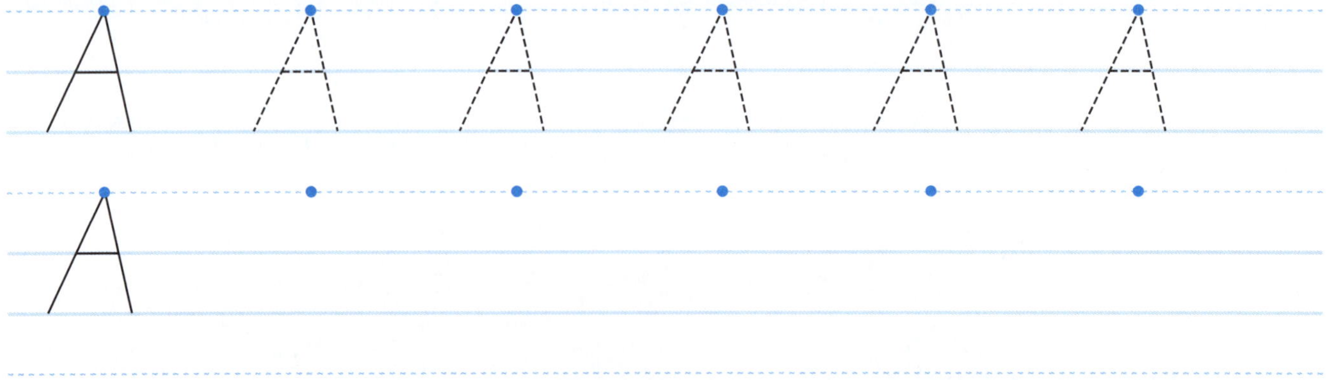

PARENT TIP: Upper-case *A* requires two pencil lifts for the three strokes. The horizontal stroke is the final stroke. Lower-case *a* is an anticlockwise letter that begins at the top right and moves to the left. It ends in a downstroke.

Trace each letter *a*.

sat mat pat sat mat

Write each letter *a*. Trace the words.

s t m t p t s t m t

Trace each letter *a*.

an all about an all

Write each letter *a*. Trace the words.

n ll bout n ll

Trace then copy the sentence.

Anaconda ate it.

Colour the picture that matches the sentence.

PARENT TIP: Explore words that rhyme with -*at* (*cat*, *bat*, *hat*, *fat*). Point out the /*a*/ sound in the middle of each word. Discuss vocabulary for the illustrations: *anaconda*, *alpaca*, *ate*. The sentence is a statement. It begins with a capital letter and ends with a full stop. Ask your child what the question might have been to get the statement as an answer: *Who ate it? What ate it?* Ask other questions about the illustrations: *When was it eaten? How was it eaten? Where ...? Did ...?*

Practice

Trace

Track the letters.

Trace then write.

Trace then write.

PARENT TIP: Point out that lower-case and upper-case c have the same shape; however, upper-case C is a tall letter. The lower-case letter c begins at the same starting point as lower-case a.

Trace each letter *c*.

cat cot cut cat cot

Write each letter *c*. Trace the words.

at ot ut at ot

Trace each letter *c*.

can call come can call

Write each letter *c*. Trace the words.

an all ome an all

Trace then copy the sentence.

Carry a camel.

Colour the picture that matches the sentence.

PARENT TIP: Explore changing the vowel sound in three-letter words beginning with the /*c*/ sound (*can*, *cap*, *cod*, *cad*, *cud*, *cup*). The word *come* is a useful spelling word that cannot be sounded out. Discuss vocabulary for the illustrations: *carry*, *camel*. Ask questions: *Is the car carrying a camel? Is the camel carrying a car?* The sentence is a command. It begins with a capital letter for the action (doing) verb *Carry*. It ends with a full stop.

Practice

Trace

Track the letters.

Trace then write.

Trace then write.

PARENT TIP: Lower-case *o* begins at the same starting point as lower-case *c* and *a*. The letter *o* looks the same as the numeral *0* (zero).

Trace each letter *o*.

pot lot not pot lot

Write each letter *o*. Trace the words.

p t l t n t p t l t

Trace each letter *o*.

one two out one two

Write each letter *o*. Trace the words.

ne tw ut ne tw

Trace then copy the sentence.

Octopus took one.

Colour the picture that matches the sentence.

PARENT TIP: Explore words that rhyme with *-ot* (*dot*, *hot*, *rot*, *cot*, *got*, *jot*). Compare the different sounds made by the letter *o* in *one*, *too*, *out*. Discuss vocabulary for the illustrations: *octopus*, *took*/*take*/*has taken*, *one*, *two*, *rock*/*rocks*. Write *rock*/*rocks* for your child. Discuss singular and plural and adding *s*. Ask the question: *How many rocks did the octopus take?* The answer is a statement. It begins with a capital letter and ends with a full stop.

Practice

Trace

Track the letters.

g G g G g G

Trace then write.

g

g

Trace then write.

G

G

PARENT TIP: Lower-case g begins like a, o and c. Make sure your child notices the similarities and differences. Upper-case G is a tall letter but it starts the same way as lower-case g and moves in an anticlockwise direction. It is made in one movement.

Trace each letter *g*.

pig dig fig pig dig

Write each letter *g*. Trace the words.

pi di fi pi di

Write each letter *g*. Trace the words.

go got give go got

Trace each letter *g*.

o ot ive o ot

Trace then copy the sentence.

Goat got grumpy.

Colour the picture that matches the sentence.

PARENT TIP: Explore words that rhyme with *-ig*. Change the middle vowel to *o* (pog, dog, fog) then *e* (*peg, deg, feg*). Talk about real and nonsense words. Discuss vocabulary for the illustrations: *goat, grumpy, giraffe*. Explore facial expressions which show *grumpy*. Discuss why a goat would be grumpy. The sentence is a statement. It begins with a capital letter and ends with a full stop.

Practice

Trace

Track the letters.

q Q q Q q Q

Trace then write.

q q q q q q

q

Trace then write.

Q Q Q Q Q Q

Q

PARENT TIP: Lower-case *q* begins at the same starting point as lower-case *a*, *c*, *d*, *g* and *o*. Have your child draw these letters on blank paper to notice the similarities. Upper-case *Q* requires a pencil lift.

Trace each letter *q*.

quiz quick quiz quick

Write each letter *q*. Trace the words.

uiz uick uiz uick

Trace each letter *q*.

quack quokka quack

Write each letter *q*. Trace the words.

uack uokka uack

Trace then copy the sentence.

It is quiet.

Colour the picture that matches the sentence.

PARENT TIP: Explore alliteration with *qu*. Point out the *qu* pattern that says /*kw*/. Point out the *ck* letter pattern and the single sound the two letters together make in *duck*, *quack*, *quick*. Discuss vocabulary for the illustrations: *duck*, *quack*, *quiet*. Point out the speech bubble and the fact that it shows what the duck is saying. The sentence is a statement. It begins with a capital letter and ends with a full stop.

Practice

d D

Trace

Track the letters.

d D d D d D

Trace then write.

d d d d d d

d

Trace then write.

D D D D D D

D

PARENT TIP: Lower-case *d* begins with an anticlockwise loop for the body of the letter and then moves up to make the tall part of the letter and down to complete the downstroke. Upper-case *D* requires a pencil lift.

Trace each letter *d*.

dad sad mad dad sad

Write each letter *d*. Trace the words.

a sa ma a sa

Trace each letter *d*.

do dip did do dip

Write each letter *d*. Trace the words.

o ip i o ip

Trace then copy the sentence.

Good dog, Dotty!

Colour the picture that matches the sentence.

PARENT TIP: Explore words that rhyme with *-ad* (*bad*, *cad*, *fab*, *tad*, *gad*). Discuss vocabulary for the illustrations: *dragon*, *Dalmatian* and the *good* behaviour of the animals in the illustrations. Point out that *Dotty* is the *dog*'s name. Names are proper nouns and so *Dotty* needs to begin with a capital letter. The sentence is an exclamation. Exclamations are said loudly or with emphasis to show surprise or excitement. The sentence begins with a capital letter and ends with an exclamation mark. Explore other examples of exclamations: *Thank you! Wow! I love it! Stop! Look out! No! Yes!*

Practice

Trace

Track the letters.

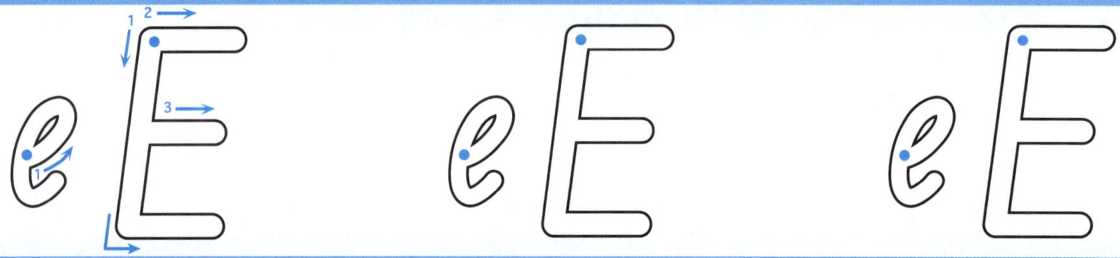

Trace then write.

Trace then write.

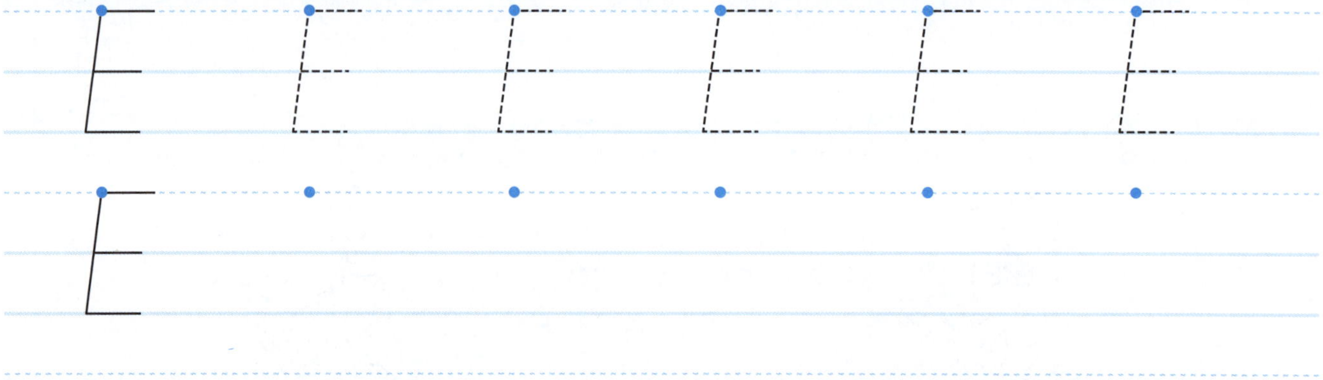

PARENT TIP: Lower-case *e* is a tricky letter to write because it starts in the middle of the letter with a line to the right and then sweeps around in an anticlockwise direction. Practise with big arm movements then make smaller wrist movements in the air. Upper-case E requires two pencil lifts. It starts like an L.

Trace each letter *e*.

wet met pet wet met

Write each letter *e*. Trace the words.

w t m t p t w t m t

Trace each letter *e*.

see sentence see sentence

Write each letter *e*. Trace the words.

s s nt nc s s nt nc

Trace then copy the sentence.

Elephant led emu.

Colour the picture that matches the sentence.

PARENT TIP: Explore words that rhyme with *-et* (*set*, *get*, *let*, *vet*, *net*, *yet*). Point out the *e* in *sentence* and the *ee* in *see*. Discuss vocabulary for the illustrations: *elephant*, *emu*. Write the words on spare paper. Compare the short /*e*/ sound in *elephant* and the long /*e*/ sound in *emu*. Talk about which animal is in the lead/first/in front and which animal is behind or second. The sentence is a statement. It begins with a capital letter and ends with a full stop.

Practice

Trace

Track the letters.

Trace then write.

Trace then write.

PARENT TIP: S is a tricky letter because it involves first an anticlockwise movement and then a change in direction to use a clockwise movement. S forms the start of the numeral 8. Wrist movements in the air will support your child's familiarity with this letter's movements.

Trace each letter *s*.

kiss hiss his kiss hiss

Write each letter *s*. Trace the words.

ki hi hi ki hi

Trace each letter *s*.

said she so said she

Write each letter *s*. Trace the words.

aid he o aid he

Trace then copy the sentence.

Some seals sat.

Colour the picture that matches the sentence.

PARENT TIP: Explore words that rhyme with -*iss*. Point out the /*z*/ sound at the end of *his*. The word *said* is useful for children's own writing. Make sure your child understands that the middle /*e*/ sound is spelt with an *ai*. Point out *said* in books you are reading with your child. Discuss vocabulary for the illustrations (*seal, some*) and the action (doing) verbs (*sit*/*sat*/*are sitting*/*splashing*). Compare the actions of the seals in the illustrations. The sentence is a statement. It begins with a capital letter and ends with a full stop.

Extra practice: anticlockwise

Trace each letter.

u v w y a c

Write each letter.

u

v

w

y

a

c

y

PARENT TIP: Have your child check their own posture, pencil grip and paper position before they start writing.

Extra practice: anticlockwise

Trace each letter.

o g q d e s

Write each letter.

o

g

q

e

d

s

q

PARENT TIP: Ask your child to tell you the similarities and differences between the letters on this page before they start writing.

Extra practice: anticlockwise

Trace each letter.

U V W Y A C

Write each letter.

U

V

W

Y

A

C

A

PARENT TIP: Have your child check their own posture, pencil grip and paper position before they start writing.

Extra practice: anticlockwise

Trace each letter.

O G Q D E S

Write each letter.

O

G

Q

D

E

S

G

PARENT TIP: Look back over previous pages and ask your child to assess for themselves which of their letters need more practice. Use spare paper if necessary.

Practice

1

one

Draw 1 spot.

Track

1 1 1 1 1

Trace then write.

1 1 1 1 1 1

1

Trace then write.

one one one one one

one

Write the missing numerals.

2 3 5 6 8 9 10

PARENT TIP: Have your child do shoulder rolls and wrist and finger stretches as a warm-up. Remind your child to hold the pencil in a relaxed grip.

Practice

2 two

Draw 2 spots.

Track

2 2 2 2 2

Trace then write.

2 2 2 2 2 2

2

Trace then write.

two two two two

two

Write the missing numerals.

1 3 5 7 8 9 10

PARENT TIP: This numeral often causes children problems. They often write it back to front. Check that your child makes one movement: begin with a clockwise curve, continue diagonally down to the main line, then make a left-to-right horizontal line.

Practice

3 three

Draw 3 spots.

Track

3 3 3 3 3

Trace then write.

3 3 3 3 3 3

3

Trace then write.

three three three three

three

Write the missing numerals.

1 2 4 5 7 8 10

PARENT TIP: This numeral often causes children problems. Children often write it back to front. Remind your child that it is a clockwise numeral.

Practice

4 four

Draw 4 spots.

Track

4 4 4 4 4

Trace then write.

4 4 4 4 4 4

4

Trace then write.

four four four four

four

Write the missing numerals.

2 3 5 6 8 9 10

PARENT TIP: Your child will have to lift the pencil off the page for the second stroke. Watch that this second stroke is parallel to the first downstroke.

Practice

5 five

Draw 5 spots.

Track

5 5 5 5 5

Trace then write.

5 5 5 5 5 5

5

Trace then write.

five five five five

five

Write the missing numerals.

2 3 4 6 7 9 10

PARENT TIP: The numeral 5 can be tricky to write. It has straight lines and a clockwise curve. It is a commonly reversed letter. It will need a pencil lift to finish with a horizontal stroke at the top. Practice makes perfect.

Practice

6 six

Draw 6 spots.

Track

6 6 6 6 6

Trace then write.

6 6 6 6 6 6

6

Trace then write.

six six six six six

six

Write the missing numerals.

1 3 5 7 8 9 10

PARENT TIP: The numeral 6 is made with one movement. Try big arm movements in the air first.

Practice

7 seven

Draw 7 spots.

Track

7 7 7 7 7

Trace then write.

7 7 7 7 7 7

7

Trace then write.

seven seven seven

seven

Write the missing numerals.

2 3 5 6 8 9 10

PARENT TIP: Do some stretching first: shoulders, arms, wrists and fingers. Point out that 7 starts at the top left, moves right and then moves down. This number is often reversed when children first start writing it.

Practice

8 eight

Track

8 8 8 8 8

Draw 8 spots.

Trace then write.

8 8 8 8 8 8

8

Trace then write.

eight eight eight eight

eight

Write the missing numerals.

2 3 4 5 7 9 10

PARENT TIP: This numeral is made without lifting the pencil. Have your child use big arm movements to make the numeral in the air before writing on paper.

Practice

Draw 9 spots.

9 nine

Track

9 9 9 9 9

Trace then write.

9 9 9 9 9 9

9

Trace then write.

nine nine nine nine

nine

Write the missing numerals.

1 3 5 6 7 8 10

PARENT TIP: The numeral 9 looks like lower-case q without the flick of the tail.

Practice

10 ten

Draw 10 spots.

Track

10 10 10 10

Trace then write.

10 10 10 10 10 10

10

Trace then write.

ten ten ten ten ten

ten

Write the missing numerals.

1 2 3 5 6 8 9

PARENT TIP: Check the elliptical shape of the 0.

Revision: lines and zigzags

Read the words.

leg lot fox leg lot

zap tap zigzag zap tap

Complete the words.

eg o o eg o

ap ap g ag ap ap

Write the word to match the picture.

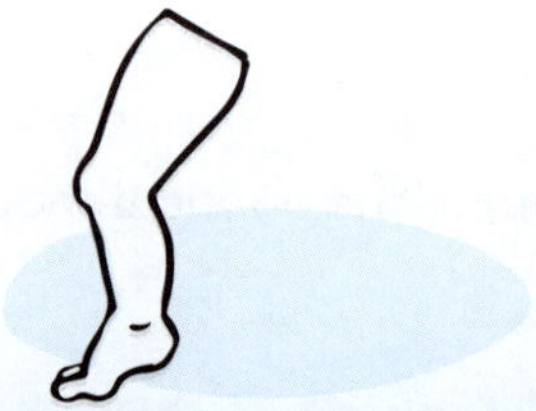

Revision: lines and zigzags

Read the words.

tip zip off tip zip

fan fin jacket fan fin

Complete the words.

p p o p p

an n acke an n

Write the word to match the picture.

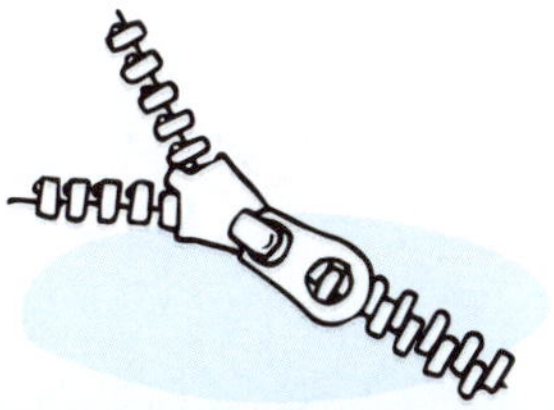

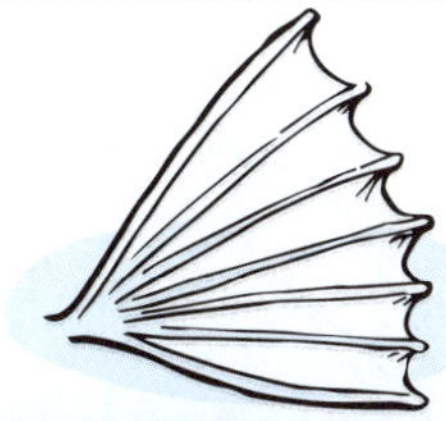

Revision: clockwise

Read the words.

kite man nap kite man

hug mat carrot hug

Complete the words.

ite a a ite a

ug at ca ot ug

Write the word to match the picture.

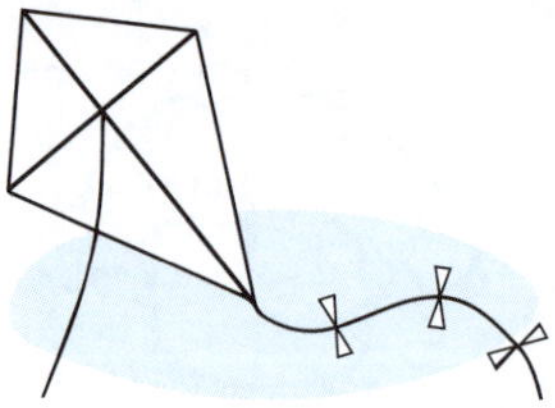

Revision: clockwise

Read the words.

map hum rocket map

bed pip pot bed pip

Complete the words.

a u oc et a

ed i ot ed i

Write the word to match the picture.

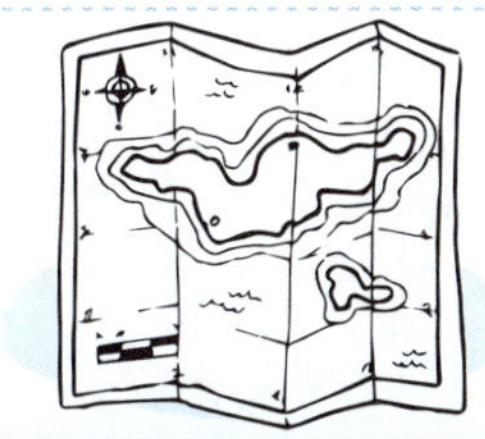

Revision: anticlockwise

Read the words.

sun yap five sun yap

web dog quilt web dog

Complete the words.

_ _ n   _ _ p   fi _ _   _ _ n   _ _ p

_ _ b   _ _ _   _ _ lt   _ _ b   _ _ _

Write the word to match the picture.

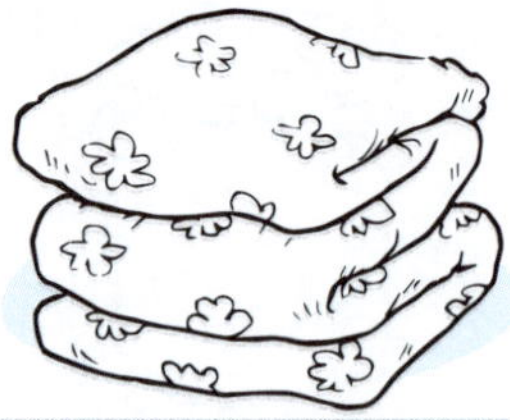

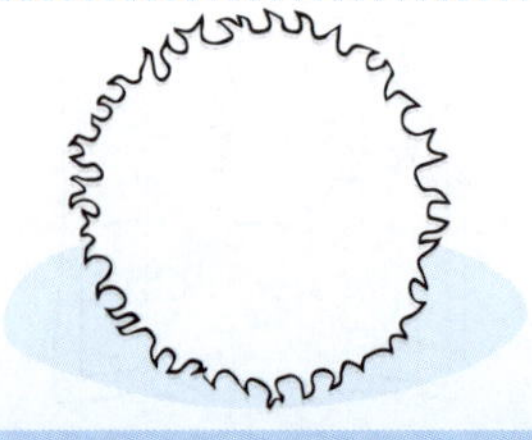

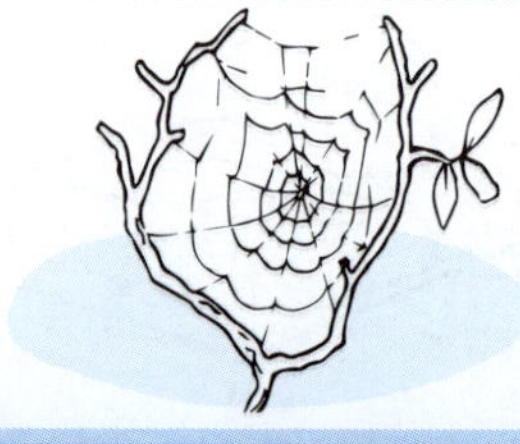

Revision: anticlockwise

Read the words.

apple cow car apple

get ant miss get ant

Complete the words.

ppl _ _ _ _ _r _ppl_

_ _t _nt mi_ _ _ _t _nt

Write the word to match the picture.

NSW Foundation Style

a b c d e f g

h i j k l m n

o p q r s t u

v w x y z

0 1 2 3 4 5

6 7 8 9 10

NSW Foundation Style

A B C D E F

G H I J K L

M N O P Q R

S T U V W

X Y Z

Posture, paper tilt and pencil grip

Posture

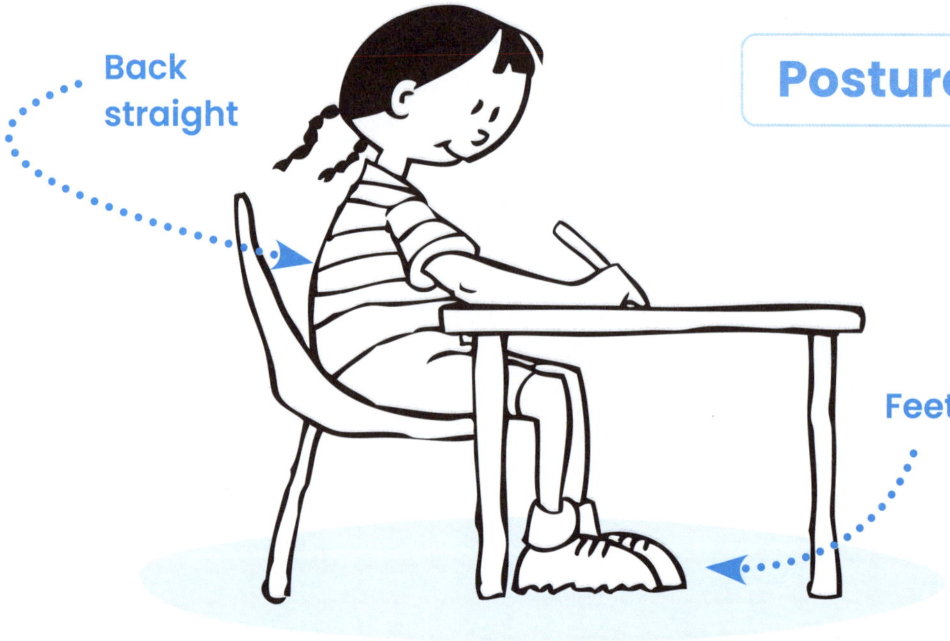

Paper tilt

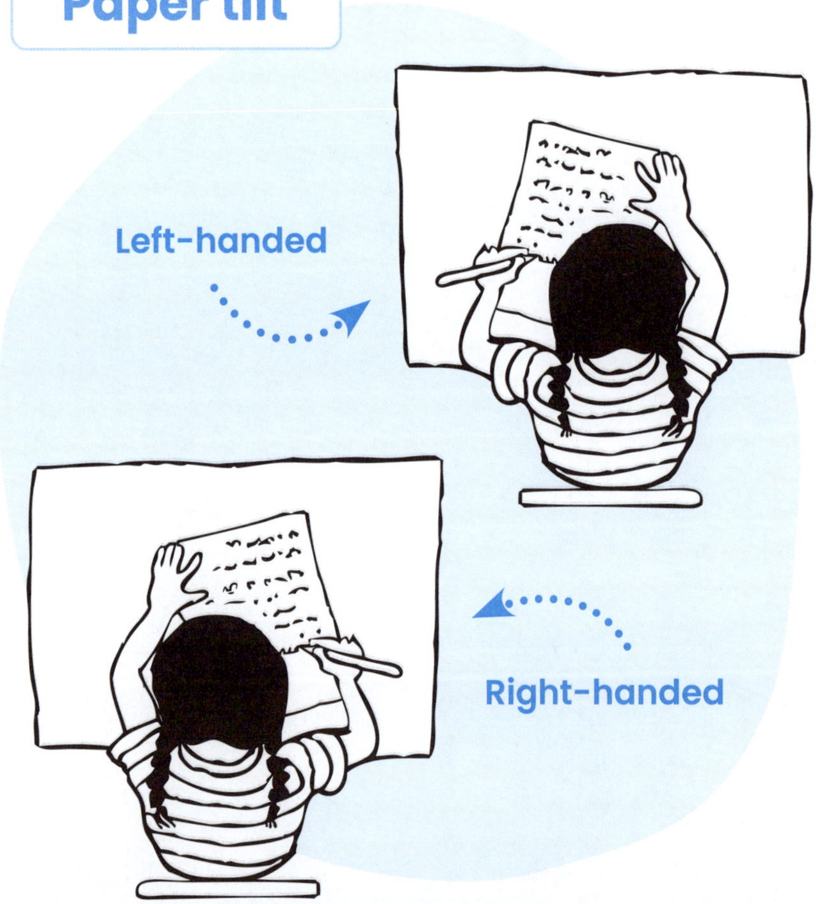

Pencil grip

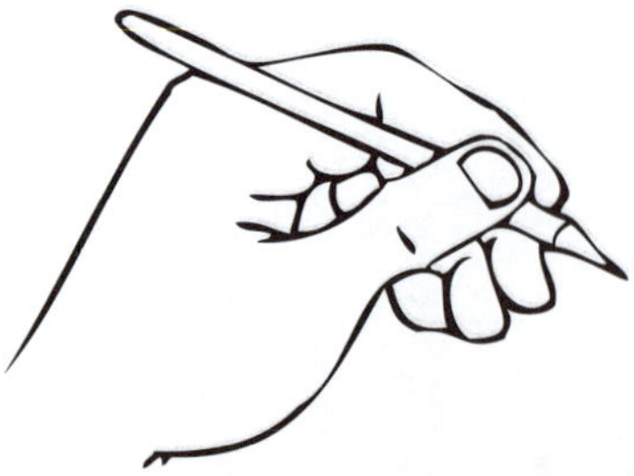

Left-handed

Right-handed